October

K. C. KELLEY • BOB OSTROM

The Child's World

Published by The Child's World®
1980 Lookout Drive • Mankato, MN 56003-1705
800-599-READ • www.childsworld.com

Acknowledgments
The Child's World®: Mary Berendes, Publishing Director
The Design Lab: Design
Jody Jensen Shaffer: Editing and Fact-Checking

Photo credits
© Alexander Hoffmann/Shutterstock.com: 6 (left); Arina P
Habich/Shutterstock.com: 13 (bottom); bikeriderlondon/
Shutterstock.com: 13 (top); CEFutcher/iStock.com: 10; chris2766/
Shutterstock.com: 11 (bottom); Dorothea Lange/Farm Security
Administration/ Office of War Information/Office of Emergency
Management/Resettlement Administration/Wikimedia Commons:
20 (top); Joachim Eckel/Dreamstime.com: 23 (bottom); John
Kropewnicki/Shutterstock.com: 22 (bottom); Leonard Zhukovsky/
Shutterstock.com: 12 (top); Library of Congress: 18l ljh images/
Shutterstock.com: 20 (bottom); Nir Levy/Shutterstock.com: 22
(top); Pach Brothers/Wikimedia Commons: 23 (middle); Phaitoon
Sutunyawatchai/Shutterstock.com: 12 (bottom); real444: iStock.
com: 6 (right); Serban Enache/Dreamstime.com: 19 (bottom);
Sergey Novikov/Shutterstock.com: cover, 1, 5; TaneeStudio/
Shutterstock.com: 11 (top); Vincent Giordano/Dreamstime.com:
23 (top); Warner Bros./Vanjagenije at en.wikipedia/Wikimedia
Commons: 19 (top)

ISBN 9781626873728
LCCN 2014930711

Printed in the United States of America
Mankato, MN
July, 2014
PA02214

ABOUT THE AUTHOR

K.C. Kelley has written dozens of books for young readers on
everything from sports to nature to history. He was born in
January, loves April because that's when baseball begins, and
loves to take vacations in August!

ABOUT THE ILLUSTRATOR

Bob Ostrom has been illustrating books for twenty years.
A graduate of the New England School of Art & Design at
Suffolk University, Bob has worked for such companies as
Disney, Nickelodeon, and Cartoon Network. He lives in North
Carolina with his wife and three children.

Contents

WELCOME TO OCTOBER!

Most kids can't wait until the end of October. That's when we celebrate Halloween, and candy fills our bags! But the rest of October is pretty great, too. Many important things have happened in history this month. Baseball season wraps up with the World Series. And many trees put on their best displays of color!

HOW DID OCTOBER GET ITS NAME?

The ancient Romans had ten months in their year. The eighth month took its name from *octo*, the Latin word for the number eight. Even after the calendar expanded to 12 months, October kept its old name.

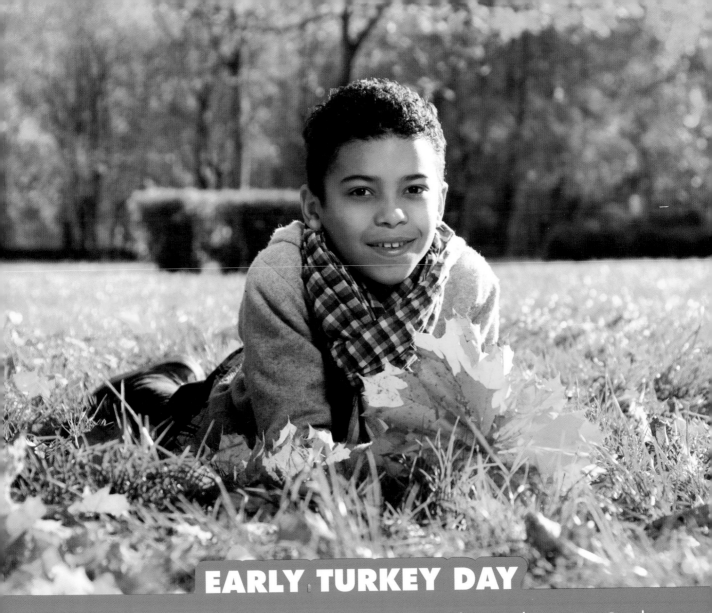

EARLY TURKEY DAY

Halloween rules October, but Thanksgiving was born this month, too. On October 3, 1863, President Abraham Lincoln made Thanksgiving a national holiday. He chose the final Thursday each November.

Birthstone

Each month has a stone linked to it. People who have birthdays in that month call it their birthstone. October has two (left to right): opal and tourmaline.

OCTOBER AROUND THE WORLD

Here is the name of this month in other languages.

Chinese	Shí yuè
Dutch	Oktober
English	October
French	Octobre
German	der Oktober
Italian	Ottobre
Japanese	Juugatsu
Spanish	Octubre
Swahili	Oktoba

LEAF PEEPERS

October is a big month for fans of beautiful fall colors in trees. In New England states, color fans are called "leaf peepers." They visit from all over to take in the sights.

BIG OCTOBER HOLIDAYS

Columbus Day, Second Monday

The United States made the second Monday in October a national holiday in 1937. This day celebrates explorer Christopher Columbus and the people who were here long before him—Native Americans. For some, Columbus Day is also a day to celebrate newcomers to the United States.

PARADE TIME

Columbus Day is the perfect excuse for a parade! Large parades are held in New York City, San Francisco, St. Louis, and other places. Since Columbus was Italian, many Italian-Americans celebrate today, too.

Halloween, October 31

The idea of Halloween came from the celebration of All Souls Day, which honors the dead. The spooky nature of death led people to celebrate life and laughter two nights before that special day. Children soon filled the streets dressed as ghosts, goblins, and ghouls to beg for treats. Candy-makers were very pleased!

WORLD SERIES

Baseball fans love October! Since 1903, the World Series has been played nearly every year in this month. The champions of baseball's American and National Leagues face off. The best-of-seven-games Series is often called The Fall Classic.

FUN OCTOBER DAYS

October has more ways to celebrate than just dressing up in your favorite costume! Here are some of the unusual holidays you can enjoy in October:

October 5

World Teachers Day

World
Egg Day

October 14

National
Dessert Day

ucato
[CE]
cated /'ɛdjʊkeɪt/ˈɛdjʊkeɪt than av
p. to a higher level (an educa
(good) education (an c
experience or study (an /'ɛdjʊ'keɪʃ(ə)/ˈɛdjʊ'keɪʃ(ə) ate
education educating or being
particular kind
ty. education; a clo
tin ter or

October 16

Dictionary Day

October 24

United Nations Day

October 25

World Pasta Day

October 27

U.S. Navy Day

October 30

National
Candy Corn
Day

OCTOBER WEEKS AND MONTHS

Holidays don't just mean days…you can celebrate for a week, too! You can also have fun all month long. Find out more about these ways to enjoy October!

OCTOBER WEEKS

Fire Prevention Week: This week reminds everyone to pay attention to fire safety.

National Metric Week: This week, scientists want people to learn more about the system. Why is October 10 always part of Metric Week? Because that date is also written as "10/10." All the metric measurements are based on the number 10!

Character Counts Week: Character means how you act and the good choices you make. Many schools take part in Character Counts programs year-round.

OCTOBER MONTHS

Children's Magazines Month: There are not as many magazines as there used to be. Many have closed. But this is a good month to check out the ones that are still doing great work. There are magazines for just about any interest you might have! Visit a newsstand and find out!

National Caramel Month: Your dentist won't like this month…but your sweet tooth will! Caramel is a sweet, sticky candy. Many people use it in baking, too.

Raptor Month: Hawks, eagles, and falcons are all a type of bird called a raptor. Find out more about these amazing animals this month. See how many types of raptors you can discover!

OCTOBER AROUND THE WORLD

Countries around the world celebrate in October. Find these countries on the map. Then read about how people there have fun in October!

Thanksgiving Day, Canada
The second Monday in October is "Turkey Day" for Canadians. It calls people together to say thanks.

EAT UP!

On October 1, celebrate World Vegetarian Day. Billions of people enjoy life without eating meat. Have you ever tried it? Then on October 16, World Food Day calls attention to people who have very little of anything to eat. Fighting hunger is one of the world's most important jobs.

Hungarian Revolution, Hungary

October 23

In 1956, Hungary was controlled by the Soviet Union. On this day, thousands of people tried to revolt to take back their country. They were quickly defeated. Today, free Hungarians remember those brave people with an important national holiday.

Health and Sports Day, Japan

Second Monday

Kids all over Japan run, jump, play, and exercise on *Taiiku no Hi*, which means "Sports Day!" The celebration was first held after the 1964 Olympics in Tokyo.

Labour Day, New Zealand

Fourth Monday

As in the U.S., New Zealand has a day that celebrates its working men and women. Like many countries that used to be part of Great Britain, the "Kiwis" spell "labour" with an added "u."

OCTOBER IN HISTORY

October 2, 1967

Thurgood Marshall was sworn to the U.S. **Supreme Court**. He was the first African-American to sit on the nation's top court.

October 4, 1957

The Soviet Union launched the first **satellite** into space. Their *Sputnik* craft launched the "space race" between the U.S. and the Soviet Union.

BIG BRITISH BATTLES

Two of the most important battles in English history were fought this month. The Battle of Hastings in 1066 ended **Saxon** rule in England. **Normans** from France took over for centuries. In 1805, Admiral Horatio Nelson led the British Navy to victory at Trafalgar, in the Atlantic Ocean. His ships defeated those from France and Spain.

October 6, 1927

The Jazz Singer, the first movie with sound, was shown in Los Angeles.

October 17, 1989

An earthquake struck San Francisco during Game 3 of the World Series. Roads and a part of a major bridge collapsed.

October 27, 1904

The first major underground subway in the U.S. opened in New York City.

October 28, 1886

The world-famous Statue of Liberty was dedicated in New York Harbor. The 305-foot (93 m) statue was cleaned up in 1986. Her golden torch now gleams again!

October 29, 1929

The **Great Depression** started when the U.S. stock market suddenly lost most of its value. Many people lost a lot of money. Some people became very poor.

October 31, 1941

Mount Rushmore was completed after 14 years of work.

NEW STATE!

Only one state joined the United States in October. Do you live in Nevada? If you do, then make sure and say, "Happy Birthday!" to your state.

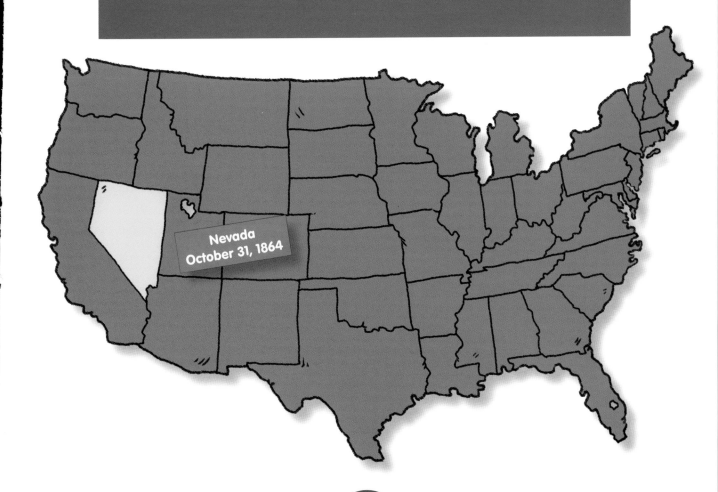

Nevada
October 31, 1864

FAMOUS OCTOBER BIRTHDAYS

October 1

Jimmy Carter

This Georgian was President of the United States from 1977–1981.

October 2

Mahatma Gandhi

This peaceful man led India to freedom from Great Britain. His nonviolent ways have inspired millions of people.

October 11

Eleanor Roosevelt

She was the wife of President Franklin D. Roosevelt, but she was also a world leader for peace and justice.

October 25

Pablo Picasso

A Spanish painter and sculptor, he was one of the 20th century's most famous artists.

October 26

Hillary Clinton

This former First Lady was also the Secretary of State and a U.S. Senator. She has also run for president.

October 27

Theodore Roosevelt

He was president from 1901–1909.

October 28

Bill Gates

The co-founder of Microsoft, Bill Gates is the world's richest person. He gives away much of his money to charities and good causes.

GLOSSARY

Great Depression (GRAYT deh-PRESH-un) A time between 1929 and about 1939 when many people faced hard economic times.

Normans (NORM-unz) A group of invaders from northern France who lived about 1,000 years ago.

raptor (RAP-tur) A bird that hunts other animals for food. Eagles and hawks are raptors.

Saxons (SAK-sunz) A group of invaders from northern Germany who lived about 1,500 years ago.

satellite (SAT-uh-lyt) Machinery that is sent into outer space to circle around Earth.

Supreme Court (soo-PREEM KORT) The Supreme Court is the highest court in the United States.

INDEX